The First Ladies
Of California

Dedicated to the first ladies in our lives, our mothers,
Josephine Beers and Charlotte Sword LaDue

The First Ladies Of California

Lynn Cook and Janet LaDue

To order additional copies of this book, contact:
Xlibris Corporation
1-888-795-4274
www.Xlibris.com
Orders@Xlibris.com
35076

Contents

Introduction 13

First Ladies

1. Harriet Rogers Burnett, 1849-1851 17
2. Jane Palmer McDougal, 1851-1852 19
3. Elizabeth Graham Bigler, 1852-1856 22
4. Mary Zabriskie Johnson, 1856-1858 25
5. Lizzie Staunton Weller, 1858-1860 28
6. Sophie Birdsall Latham, January 9, 1860-January 14, 1860 31
7. Maria Guirado Downey, 1860-1862 34
8. Jane Elizabeth Lathrop Stanford, 1862-1863 37
9. Mollie Creed Low, 1863-1867 40
10. Anna Bissell Haight, 1867-1871 43
11. Bachelor in office, Newton Booth, 1871-1875
    Married Octavia Glover,1892, no children
12. Mary McIntyre Pacheco, February 27, 1875-December 9, 1875 46
13. Amelia Cassidy Irwin, 1875-1880 49
14. Ruth Parker Perkins, 1880-1883 52
15. Mary Hardisty Stoneman, 1883-1887 55
16. Bachelor in office, Washington Bartlett,
    January 8, 1887-September 12,1887
17. Jane Gardner Waterman, 1887-1891 59
18. Mary Dana Markham, 1891-1895 62
19. Inez Merrill Budd, 1895-1899 65
20. Francisca "Fannie" Victoria Rains Gage, 1899-1903 68
21. Helen Penniman Pardee, 1903-1907 72
22. Isabella Erzgraber Gillette, 1907-1911 75
23. Minnie L. McNeal Johnson, 1911-1917 78
24. Flora Rawson Stephens, 1917-1923 81

25. Augusta Fielder Richardson, 1923-1927 84
26. Lyla Vincent Young, 1927-1931 87
27. Annie Reid Rolph, 1931-1934 90
28. Jessie Stewart Merriam, 1936-1939 93
29. Kate Jeremy Olson, January, 1939-April, 1939 96
30. Nina Palmquist Warren, 1943-1953 100
31. Virginia Carlson Knight, 1954-1959 103
32. Bernice Layne Brown, 1959-1967 106
33. Nancy Davis Reagan, 1967-1975 110
34. Bachelor in Office, Edmund G. "Jerry" Brown, 1975-1983
    Married Anne Gust June 18, 2005
35. Gloria Saatjian Deukmejian, 1983-1991 113
36. Gayle Edlund Wilson, 1991-1999 116
37. Sharon Ryer Davis, 1999-2003 119
38. Maria Shriver Schwarzenegger, 2003— 122

Bibliography 125
Endnotes 131

Disclaimer

This research was done in its entirety by the two of us and represents a year and a half of work. Our goal in writing this book was to be as historically accurate as possible. We found this to be difficult with some of the early first ladies because of the lack of information or the misinformation. For instance, different sources reported different dates for births, marriages, or deaths. Family records were sometimes destroyed or not kept at all.

Because of these circumstances, we apologize if any of the information is not correct and hope that any descendents or family will contact us so we can make the changes in future revisions.

Lynn Cook and Janet LaDue

Acknowledgements

Janet LaDue and Lynn Cook would like to thank the following people:

My husband Jack Cook for his help and support during this whole project.

Special thanks to former First Ladies: Mrs.Gloria Deukmejian, Mrs. Gayle Wilson, and Mrs. Sharon Davis. Thank you to Wren Powell, Executive Assistant to Mrs. Nancy Reagan, and Trish Fontana, Director of Special Projects for Mrs. Maria Shriver Schwarzenegger.

Bissell Mansion Restaurant and Dinner Theater, 4426 Randall Place, St. Louis, Missouri.

Kimberly D. Bowden, Curator of Archival Collections, The Haggin Museum, Stockton, California.

California State Capitol Museum Volunteer Association, California State Capitol, Sacramento, California.

Lorraine Donnelly, author of *Capitol Historical Rooms, and* State Capitol volunteer docent.

Clare Ellis and Nancy Phillips, Librarians; Sacramento Public Library, Sacramento Room, Sacramento, California.

Joseph Evans, California Historical Society, San Francisco, California.

Wendy Franklin, State Park Interpreter III; and Larry Bishop, Park Interpretive Specialist; California State Parks Historical Sites, Sacramento, California.

Kathy Fotopoulos, a trainer of the new docent class and a docent at the State Capitol, who encouraged us to start this project.

Nathan D. Gonzales, Ph.D., Associate Archivist, A. K. Smiley Public Library, Redlands, California.

Patricia Keats, Library Director, Society of California Pioneers, San Francisco, California.

David Kessler, Bancroft Library, University of California, Berkeley, California.

Richard Kimball, Native Sons of the Golden West, San Francisco, California.

Gary F. Kurutz and the staff at the California State Library: Janet Clemmensen, Kathy Correla, Michael Dolgushkin, John Gonzales, Kira Graybill, Catherine Hanson-Tracy, Jenny Hoye, Vickie Lockhart, Vicky Newton, Karen Paige, Sarah Rowland, Kelisha Skoglund, Bill Waterman.

Latter Day Saints, Multi-Stake Family History Center, 2745 Eastern Avenue, Sacramento, California.

Mary Lou Lentz, for valuable guidance to Sacramento historical resources.

Michael Maher, Chris Driggs, Nevada Historical Society, Reno, Nevada.

Dan McLaughlin, Librarian I, D. Mendez References Services, Pasadena Public Library, Pasadena, California.

Mercer County Historical Society, Mercer, Pennsylvania.

Missouri State Archives, St. Louis, Missouri.

David Nicolai, Museum Director, Pardee Mansion, 672 Eleventh Street, Oakland, California.

Judy Russo, Mike Tucker and Mike Bush, California Archives, West Sacramento, California.

Debbie Mastel Scott, San Joaquin County Historical Museum, Lodi, California.

Dr. James Sewell and Bill Philson, Mercer County Historical Museum, Mercer, Pennsylvania.

Vito Sgromo, State of California Department of General Services, California Sate Capitol, Sacramento, California.

Siskiyou County Historical Society, Yreka, California.

Sean Stewart, San Diego Historical Society, San Diego, California.

Jason Stratman, Assistant Librarian, Missouri Historical Society, St. Louis, Missouri.

Pamela Struck, John Rains House, National Register of Historic Homes, Rancho Cucamonga, California.

Michael Whitely, Dorothy Lindsey, and Peggy Adamson, Butte County Historical Society, Oroville, California.

Introduction

Years ago, as today, each first lady had many responsibilities: supportive wife and mother, active in community service, a model in decorum and etiquette, and at all times, be the diplomat. She had to be first in the social world as well as first in service to the state. As first lady, she had to become accustomed to hearing negative criticism of her husband and had to give up family privacy. Then, like now, there were scandals and personal business that could make the family uncomfortable.

In early California, there were very few women, about eight women for every hundred men. Women were held in the highest esteem, and it was said that the pioneer women had more freedom and mobility than in later years. That being said, women were thought to be more important in social affairs rather than in business or politics. Pioneer women endured many hardships, had very little in the way of entertainment, their main job being a companion to their husbands and mother to their children.

Researching the early first ladies, we found how unimportant the role of women was. Many obituaries of the early governors did not mention their wives' names, stating that he left a wife and a child or children. If the first lady's obituary was found, it may not address her first name but refer to her as Mrs. Governor, describing her as being devoted to her husband, dignified, and a gracious hostess. Appearance and clothing seemed to be most important. The dresses were described in detail, particularly, the inaugural ball gowns. Although we may question this, even today, you will find many articles describing the clothes worn, for instance, at the Academy Awards.

Because the state was fairly uncivilized, the women had an opportunity to establish morality, culture, family life, and values. In California, women obtained the right to vote in 1911. Nationally, women did not get the vote until 1920.

The first ladies were primarily social leaders and supporters of their husbands. A new responsibility for a first lady was when the state gave Helen Pardee, 1903-1907, a household budget. Being the first family to move into the Governor's Mansion, Helen Pardee was told that she had to buy all the furniture and household goods. When each first lady moved into the mansion, she learned that all furnishings and household items were state property. Each knew that some of her decisions and tastes may be criticized, and she could be labeled as too thrifty or too extravagant. One of the many duties of the first lady was to make a temporary house into a pleasant and happy home for the family.

It is interesting to note that well into the 1960's, most of the ladies wanted to be a full-time wife and mother. Although each lady had official duties, an office at the Capitol was not provided until Mrs. Gayle Wilson was first lady, 1991-1998.

While researching the first ladies, we found each made a difference and believe she deserves to be remembered in the history of California.

"Being First Lady is an extraordinary opportunity to make a difference. I hope in some small way that is what I have done."

Former First Lady Sharon Davis, 1999-2003

Letter to Mrs. Rice from Mabel A. Burnett (Mrs. David M. Burnett)

My Dear Mrs. Rice:

At long last I am sending you the information you asked concerning David's dear grandmother, Mrs. Peter H. Burnett.

I am sorry to be so late, but we have been trying to get a photograph other than the daguerreotype which all the family has always felt was most uncomplimentary to the dear little lady. All of her grandchildren remember her as most sweet and attractive and like to think of her that way.

The Governor in his "Memoirs" was most complimentary and affectionate and I quote him as writing: She was a little above medium height, with a trim figure, sparkling black eyes, handsome face, low sweet voice and gentle manners." So we will forget the daguerreotype! . . . .[1]

First Lady Harriet Rogers Burnett
1849-1851

FIRST GOVERNOR, PETER BURNETT

Harriet Rogers was a pioneer first lady who traveled across the country by wagon train. She was a pretty, petite and religious woman with strong convictions and common sense. In 1811, Harriet was born in Wilson County, Tennessee.

At the age of seventeen, Harriet married Peter Burnett on August 20, 1828. The first year of marriage, they had a twenty-five-dollar-a-year income. When Harriet's sister and her husband, Burnett's older brother, moved to Missouri, Peter sent Harriet and their infant son to live there.

Later, the family now with six children—Dwight, Martha Letitia, Romietta, John, Armstead, and Sallie—left Weston, Missouri, to travel west. At the time, Harriet, being in poor health, was told by the doctor that the trip "would kill her or cure her."[2] Traveling to Oregon in two oxen wagons and two small horse wagons at an average speed of eleven and a half miles per day, they reached Fort Walla Walla, Washington, on October 16, 1843. They had traveled 1,691 miles.

The family moved many times, first settling in Fort Vancouver, then moving to Oregon City in May, 1844. At this time, Peter joined the Catholic Church. The rest of the family was Protestant, including Harriet, who was quite religious.

When gold was discovered in California, Burnett moved his family, who made the trip by sailing and arriving in San Francisco on June 1, 1849.

The family moved again, this time to San Jose, because they thought their daughter was dying of consumption. Eventually, the daughter recovered.

That same year, when Peter Burnett was elected governor, the capitol was in San Jose. Governor Burnett had owned property in Sacramento, which he sold for fifty thousand dollars, a fortune in those days, and built a spacious new home in Alviso, a city near San Jose. Four years later, he had the house dismantled and moved back to San Jose.

In 1857, Peter and Harriet took their first ocean voyage around the Horn to New York. Later, they traveled to Missouri to visit family and friends. They lived in San Jose and San Francisco until Harriet died on September 19, 1879. Peter died on May 17, 1895.

First Lady Jane Palmer McDougal 1851–1852

SECOND GOVERNOR, JOHN MCDOUGAL

Excerpts from Mrs. McDougal's diary on her return trip beginning May 1, 1849:

May 1, 1849, Tuesday morning. This is the day we are to bid adieu to San Francisco. With the exception of leaving my husband and three or four friends, I confess I leave without regret. This morning is very gloomy and unpleasant . . . .

May 8, Tuesday . . . . The motion of the ship with the swell of the sea makes me very sick. Run 235 miles in the last twenty-four hours.

May 9, Wednesday . . . . We spent a very pleasant day. Were delighted with Mazatlan but felt very glad to get back to the ship, for home, be it ever so humble, is still home, and we consider the ship as such until we leave her in Panama . . . .

> May 16, Wednesday. Today I am twenty-five years old. A birthday on the Pacific, more than I had ever expected and may I be off it before I am a week old . . . .

> May 17, Thursday . . . . I have been sewing all day, and the time passes as pleasantly as it is possible under all the circumstances . . . .[3]

There is little known of Jane Palmer's early life. What is known is that Jane Palmer was born on May 16, 1824, in Indiana. She was the daughter of Nathan and Chloe Sackett Palmer. Jane Palmer and John McDougal were married on July 13, 1841.

In 1848, John McDougal decided to join his brother George in Sacramento, California. John booked passage for himself, Jane, and their four-year-old daughter Sue on the *Falcon*. The *Falcon* sailed from New Orleans on December 18, 1848, and arrived in Panama on December 27, 1848. The California-bound passengers crossed the Isthmus and arrived in Panama City, Panama. On February 1, 1849, the *California* left on its maiden voyage to San Francisco. Of the 364 passengers, 14 were women, one being Jane McDougal.

The *California* arrived in San Francisco, California, on February 28, 1849. Being unsuccessful in the gold mines, John McDougal began to manage his brother's store in Sutterville. During this time, Mrs. McDougal was unhappy with her home and "compelled by personal and unforeseen circumstances"[4] to return to Indiana. She booked passage on the *California* to Panama with her brother-in-law, daughter Sue, and a servant named Turner. They began their return trip on May 1, 1849. On this trip, Jane McDougal kept her journal.

Mrs. McDougal wrote of practical jokes, horseplay, and mock trials as favorite pastimes, as well as amateur theaters, teas, parties, and songfests. She also wrote of seasickness, bad food, and poor weather as being some of the more unpleasant experiences of the trip. Included in her journal were descriptions of the towns and villages of Panama and Mexico. Many days Mrs. McDougal spent sewing, mending, and being with friends.

About 1852, Mrs. McDougal returned to California over the Nicaragua route on the *North Star*. The *North Star* was shipwrecked when she ran aground fifty miles south of Acapulco. Before reaching land, the passengers suffered greatly.

Mrs. McDougal died in 1862, giving birth to a premature daughter, Elizabeth.

Elizabeth Bigler's Gravesite, Sacramento City Cemetery, 2006 Photo by Janet LaDue

First Lady Elizabeth Graham Bigler
1852-1856

THIRD GOVERNOR, JOHN BIGLER

Elizabeth R. Graham, another pioneer lady who traveled across the United States, was born in Pennsylvania about 1806. It is unclear when Elizabeth met John Bigler, who was raised in Mercer County, Pennsylvania. In 1846, John Bigler gave up his printing business in Pittsburgh and moved to Illinois. On April 2, 1849, John, Elizabeth, and their only daughter, Virginia, left Mount Sterling, Illinois, to travel by oxcart across the country to California.

Before they started their trip, Mrs. Bigler had a son who died in childbirth. Despite her weak condition, Elizabeth helped drive the wagon. According to the daughter, Virginia "Jennie" Cummings, the trip was very difficult for the family and was made even more difficult when Jennie broke a "limb."

When the family arrived in Sacramento, John was penniless and worked at different jobs to feed his family. When he worked for a merchant, in addition to his wages, he was given enough calico fabric for his wife to make dresses.

After John was elected lieutenant governor, the Bigler home became a social center, Jennie being a favorite in Sacramento society. Elizabeth was her husband's "constant companion and helpmate."[5] After John Bigler completed his second term as governor, he became the United States minister to Chile. The family left Sacramento and returned in 1861.

Virginia, or Jennie, married Andrew Cummings at the family home on September 23, 1871.

Within a two-year period, the entire family died. John Bigler died on November 29, 1871, soon after Jennie was married. Jennie, their only daughter, passed away February 5, 1873. That same year on November 15, Elizabeth died suddenly at the age of sixty-seven. She was living in the family's Sacramento residence on H Street between Eleventh and Twelfth.

John, Elizabeth, and Virginia were buried in the Sacramento City Cemetery. John and Elizabeth were members of the Sacramento Society of California Pioneers. The Biglers left no descendents.

J. Neely Johnson House, Sacramento,
2006 Photo by Janet LaDue

First Lady Mary Zabriskie Johnson
1856–1858

FOURTH GOVERNOR, J. NEELY JOHNSON

Mary Brevoort Zabriskie was the accomplished daughter of Colonel James C. Zabriskie, a lawyer and a member of the well-known Polish colonial family of Zabriskies of California, formerly of New Jersey. Mary Zabriskie and Colonel J. Neely Johnson were married on June 26, 1851, in San Francisco, California, by Reverend Benton. They had one son and one daughter.

J. Neely Johnson was elected California's fourth governor on September 5, 1855, and inaugurated on January, 1856. California's preceding governors, Peter Burnett, John McDougal, and John Bigler, did not have inaugural balls. J. Neely Johnson's inaugural ball was California's first and held in the Forest Theater. The ball was considered one of Sacramento's most elegant events of its time. The Forest Theater was decorated with gaslights, beautifully gowned women, and lively music. The chef d' cuisine was Monsieur Raynald, who designed four or five tables with food of every description and delicacy. "Pyramids of confectionery"[6] centerpieces were admired by the crowd. Guests danced until sunup.

As the wife of the governor, Mary Johnson was one of the most beautiful women on the Pacific Coast. She was vivacious and charming, a leader in society, and well remembered in Sacramento. She had a large circle of friends and was a woman of high breeding and intellect.

Early in 1869, they moved to Washoe, Nevada, where J. Neely Johnson was in charge of the Bowers mines and then continued his law practice in Carson City, Nevada. Upon the death of ex-Governor Johnson, Mary Johnson married Colonel Sylvester H. Day and resided nearly twenty-seven years in Carson City, Nevada. She passed away in Carson City, Nevada, on November 23, 1887, of heart disease after a very short illness.

INAUGURATION BALL.—The preparation for the Inauguration Ball were fully completed yesterday prior to the hour for the commencement of the festivities. The National Theater, which was selected for the fete' is certainly admirably adapted to the purpose. The stage and the parquet having been floored over, the flooring covered with canvas, and every obstruction removed, presented a clear area of about ninety feet in length by fifty feet in width. A beautiful cavern scene from "Aladdin" furnished the background; others scarely inferior in artistic merit were arranged at the sides, and the dress circle and supporting columns were festooned with ever greens, presenting certainly a pleasing and inviting appearance. A portion of the house was appropriately portioned off for a ladies dressing room, and provided with a stove to counteract the winter air. The music for the occasion (a guaranty of its acceptable quality) was furnished by the Sacramento Union Brass Band—Mr. Parsons leading the brass, and Mr. Wyatt the string instruments. If the occasion was not generally enjoyed by the participants, it cannot be attributed to any deficiency in this respect.

Wellers' Inauguration Ball Article
Sacramento Union, January, 1858

First Lady Lizzie Staunton Weller
1858–1860

FIFTH GOVERNOR, JOHN WELLER

Mrs. G. W. "Lizzie" Staunton, married Honorable John B. Weller on June 20, 1854, at the Calvary Church in New York. Reverend Dr. Hawkes performed the ceremony. Lizzie, formerly Elizabeth Winoma Brocklebank, was the youngest daughter of Levi Brocklebank, Esq., of Canada West. This was the second marriage for Lizzie and the fourth marriage for John Weller. At that time, John Weller was serving in the United States Senate from California.

At an early age, John had married Miss Ryan, who lived but a short time after they were married. Early in his congressional career, John married Miss Bryan, whose father was auditor of the state of Ohio. She died two years after they were married. In 1845, he married Miss Taylor, a niece of Thomas H. Benton, senator from Missouri. They had one child, John B. Weller Jr. Three years later, she died.

Little is known of Lizzie Staunton, who became John Weller's fourth wife. She was born in New York about 1828. The date Lizzie met John is unknown.

John Weller purchased a house in Sacramento on May 14, 1855. In 1857, he finished his term in Congress, and John and Lizzie returned to Sacramento.

Lizzie was a stepmother to John B. Weller Jr. and had five servants working in the house. In 1858, John Weller was elected governor. That same year, Lizzie and John Weller had one child, Charles Weller.

After his term of governor was completed, John was appointed a minister to Mexico. The Wellers lived a short time in Alameda, California, on a beautiful homestead of 117 acres. In 1867, John Weller and the family moved to New Orleans, where John died of smallpox on August 17, 1875. When John Weller died, he left two children: John and Charles. There is no mention of Lizzie, and it is not known where and when Lizzie died.

First Lady Sophie Latham,
Courtesy of California State Library

Courtesy of the Society of California Pioneers,
Sherman Music Collection

First Lady Sophie Birdsall Latham
January 9, 1860-January 14, 1860

SIXTH GOVERNOR, MILTON SLOCUM LATHAM

Sophie Birdsall was the eldest daughter of Lewis A. Birdsall, Esq. On the morning of October 1, 1853, before Milton Slocum Latham was to leave by steamer to take his seat in Congress, Sophie Birdsall and Milton Latham were united in marriage. The wedding ceremony was performed in San Francisco, California, by the Honorable Solomon Hyderfeldt at the home of John McDougal.

Mrs. Milton Latham was known as the "Belle of the Prairie".[7] She was a great favorite in the early society of Sacramento and San Francisco, California. Mrs. Latham had a superior mind, charming character, was well accomplished, and well fitted to be Milton Latham's companion for life. He was very devoted to her. They had no children. The inaugural ball was held on January 10, 1860, at the Pavilion in Sacramento. People from Sacramento, San Francisco, and the surrounding mining towns attended. The music was excellent with dancing continuing until four in the morning.

On January 11, 1860, after being California's governor for five days, Governor Latham resigned. He had been elected to the United States Senate to fill the vacancy caused by the death of Senator David Broderick, who had been killed in a duel. Mr. Latham moved to Washington, D.C. Mrs. Latham followed when her health improved. They lived in Washington, D.

C., until March, 1863. After not being reelected to the Senate, they moved back to San Francisco where Mr. Latham continued his law practice.

Mrs. Latham died on September 10, 1867, in their home on Folsom Street in San Francisco. Milton Latham had a monument built in her honor at Laurel Hill Cemetery in San Francisco.

First Lady Maria Downey
Courtesy of California Historical Society

First Lady Maria Guirado Downey
1860-1862

SEVENTH GOVERNOR, JOHN DOWNEY

The Guirado family was one of the oldest and most distinguished early California families. In 1833, Don Rafael Guirado, a Spanish gentleman from Guaymas, Mexico, settled in the area of Whittier. Being a very educated man, Don Rafael became an influential citizen in Los Angeles. Dona Maria Jesus Guirado was born as the only daughter in the family of three brothers. In 1852, Maria married John Gately Downey, who was born in Ireland. John Downey had arrived in San Francisco with ten dollars in his pocket. He moved to Los Angeles, started a drugstore, and then a bank. He bought land and started the town of Downey.

Maria is described as educated, refined, beautiful, and a talented woman. As first lady, she was a model for dignity and grace and liked to help the more unfortunate as one of her duties. John Downey was "devotedly attached, with all the ardor of his nature to his wife."[8] According to her obituary, "She was a woman whose whole life was devoted to her husband, and every thought seemed to be centered on him."[9]

After John Downey served as governor, Maria and he moved to Los Angeles where he built a two-story brick mansion including the first private ballroom in town. The former Maria Guirado and he gave elegant parties that made them very important in Southern California society.

On January 29, 1883, returning from a nephew's wedding in San Francisco, Maria and he were in a train wreck. The train stopped in the

Tehachapi Mountains. When the engine was detached to take on water, the train started to move and rolled over in a canyon. The oil lamps and stoves set fire to the cars. Although John Downey survived, there were twenty people who were killed including his wife Maria Guirado Downey. They had no children.

John Downey married Rose Kelly in 1888, who died in 1892. John Downey died on March 1, 1894.

First Lady Jane Stanford
Courtesy of California State Library

Stanford Mansion, Sacramento, 2006 Photo by Janet LaDue

First Lady Jane Elizabeth Lathrop Stanford
1862-1863

EIGHTH GOVERNOR, LELAND STANFORD

Jane Lathrop grew up in a well-to-do home in Albany, New York. The daughter of Dyer and Jane Shields Lathrop was born on August 25, 1828, the third of seven children. Jane Lathrop was educated at the Albany Female Academy. She had never been away from home and was deeply attached to her parents.

Jane Lathrop met Leland Stanford when he became an apprentice in a law office in Albany, New York. Before he left Albany to set up his law office in Port Washington, Wisconsin, they became engaged. They were married on September 30, 1850. When Leland Stanford sailed for California, Mrs. Stanford stayed in Albany to care for her ill father until he passed away on April 19, 1855. Leland returned to New York, and they sailed from New York, arriving in San Francisco on November 16, 1855.

The Stanfords moved to Sacramento and eventually purchased their home on Eighth and N Streets, where they entertained frequently. When Mrs. Stanford was first lady, she established a new rule of etiquette where she would expect the first call from ladies visiting Sacramento. In February, 1872, they hosted a brilliant ball in honor of Governor Newton Booth and members of the legislature. Other visitors to the Stanford Mansion were United States Secretary of State Seward, President and Mrs. Hayes, his Secretary of War Alexander Ramsey, and General Sherman.

On May 14, 1868, the Stanfords became the parents of their only child, Leland Stanford Jr. Leland Jr. was the light of his parents' lives, energetic and inquisitive. At the age of fifteen, while visiting Florence, Italy, Leland Stanford Jr. contracted typhoid fever. Despite the best medical care, he passed away on March 13, 1884. In memory of their only child, the Stanfords endowed Leland Stanford Junior University in Palo Alto, California. In October, 1891, Leland Stanford Junior University opened its doors. Jane Stanford continued to oversee its operation until her death on February 28, 1905, in Honolulu, Hawaii. Some believe there were suspicious circumstances about her death. She was buried on the Stanford campus with her husband and son.

First Lady Mollie Low
Courtesy of California State Library

Mrs. F.F.L. wore a superb toilette habillee of Chambry gauze; over this a charming Figaro jacket, made of mohair, or horsehair, or something of that kind; over this again a Raphael blouse of cheveux de la reine, trimmed round the bottom with lozenges formed of insertions, and around the top with bronchial torches; nothing could be more graceful than the contrast between the lozenges and the roches; over the blouse she wore a robe de chambre of regal magnificence, made of Faille silk and ornamented with macaroon (usually spelled "maccaroni") buttons set in black guipure. On the the roof of her bonnet was a menagerie of rare and beautiful bugs and reptiles, and under the eves thereof a counterfeit of the "early bird" whose specialty it hath been to work destruction upon such things since time began. To say that Mrs. L. was never more elaborately dressed in her life, would be to express an opinion within the range of possibility, at least-to say that she did or could look otherwise than charming, would be a deliberate departure from the truth.[10]

Mark Twain's Newspaper Article Describing Mollie Low's Dress

First Lady Mollie Creed Low
1863-1867

NINTH GOVERNOR, FREDERICK LOW

Mary Mollie Livering Creed met Frederick Low in Marysville, California. She was born on January 17, 1840, in Lancaster, Ohio. Mollie moved to Marysville, California, where she lived with an aunt and uncle. Frederick Low had moved to Marysville after his San Francisco business was destroyed by fire. They were married at the Methodist Church in Marysville on December 22, 1857. Flora Low, their only child, was born the following year. When Frederick Low was elected governor, the family moved into the Stanford Mansion on December 10, 1863. At the time, Flora was five years old.

The new first lady was described as a beautiful and a gracious hostess, entertaining and taking a prominent place in society. At an early age, Mollie's hair had turned white which made for a striking and attractive contrast to her youthful face. In publications of that era, fashions were described in detail. Mark Twain wrote a description of Mrs. Low's dress worn to the Lick House Ball in September 27, 1863.

After leaving office, Low was appointed minister to China. Low and his family set sail to China in February, 1870. "The living conditions for the diplomat and his family were most Spartan."[11] On November 20, Mrs. Low arranged an important diplomatic state dinner, half American and half Chinese. Some of the ladies and she watched unobserved from another room.

In 1874, the family returned to San Francisco. Ten years later, the family decided to travel, taking a yearlong journey around the world. On another trip to a spa in Germany, they met with Jane and Leland Stanford. At that time, Jane inquired about Frederick's health. Flora told Jane Stanford that her mother said, "When your father can get off his jokes and stories at seven o'clock in the morning, you know your father is himself again."[12]

Although Molly Low would have preferred to live in Europe, she lived the rest of her life in San Francisco, being an important part of San Francisco society. Frederick Low died on July 21, 1894. Mollie Low died on October 1, 1910, in her apartments at the St. Francis Hotel and was buried at Cypress Lawn Cemetery.

First Lady Anna Haight
Courtesy of California Historical Society

First Lady Anna Bissell Haight
1867-1871

TENTH GOVERNOR, HENRY HUNTLY HAIGHT

Anna Bissell was the daughter of Captain Lewis Bissell of St. Louis, Missouri. The St. Louis, Missouri, 1850 census shows Lewis Bissell with a daughter, Anna, sixteen years old. There is no actual date of her birth, but she was probably born in 1834. Lewis Bissell came from an impressive family of American military leaders. The Bissell Mansion, one of the oldest homes in St. Louis, Missouri, was built by Captain Lewis Bissell in the mid-1820's. Anna Bissell met Henry Huntly Haight, Esq., of San Francisco, California, in St. Louis, Missouri. In a letter dated February 12, 1855, to his friend Doughtery, Lewis Bissel states that Anna "entered in a life partnership with Henry H. Haight (a California lawyer) on the 24th of last month."[13] Lewis Bissell continues to state that the couple left for California the next day. They were to sail from New York on February 5, but were delayed by a snowstorm. Mr. and Mrs. Haight telegraphed New York to transfer their tickets for a February 20 sailing. They were the parents of one daughter and two sons.

Mrs. Haight had a wide circle of friends and was a lady of many excellent qualities. She presided in the Governor's Mansion with grace and dignity. The Haight family was among the oldest members of the First Presbyterian Church on Stockton and Clay Streets in San Francisco.

Mrs. Haight passed away in Oakland, California, on March 29, 1898, at the age of sixty-five. She had been in failing health since the death of ex-Governor Haight four years earlier. She was survived by their three children. The cause of death was heart failure. Mrs. Haight was buried in Mountain View Cemetery in Oakland, California.

First Lady Mary Pacheco
Courtesy of California State Library

Courtesy of *Wave* Magazine, September 26, 1891

First Lady Mary McIntyre Pacheco
February 27, 1875-December 9, 1875

TWELFTH GOVERNOR, ROMUALDO PACHECO

Mary McIntyre was the daughter of an old Kentucky family of Scotch-Irish lineage. She was born in Danville, Kentucky, on January 2, 1842, and was educated in Madison, Indiana, and Baltimore, Maryland.

On Saturday afternoon on October 31, 1863, the Honorable Romualdo Pacheco, state treasurer, married his own "treasure,"[14] Mary McIntyre, in San Francisco, California. The ceremony was performed in the chamber of St. Mary's Cathedral. Mr. and Mrs. Pacheco left that afternoon for Sacramento, California. Maybella Romona was born in 1865, in San Francisco, California; and a son, Romualdo Jr., was born later and died at age seven.

Mrs. Pacheco was a brilliant conversationalist and a natural leader. She was described as one of the last of the great hostesses. She continued in San Francisco and in Sacramento the traditions of the best in literary salons.

Mrs. Pacheco was among the first women writers in California. Her first published novel was titled *Montablan* A few years later, Mrs. Pacheco wrote the comedy farce *Incog*. It is said to be one of the first comedies written by a woman. *Incog* contained humor and wit and had a long run in New York and in London. *Nothing But Money* followed and achieved similar success. Mrs. Pacheco's interest in the theater also extended to theatrical productions. Governor Pacheco lost a large amount of his fortune financing his wife's theatrical productions.

Mrs. Pacheco died suddenly at the Kellogg Apartments in San Francisco, California, on November 5, 1913, at the age of seventy-one. Mrs. Pacheco had been in good health until her final illness. She had recently visited New York. Four days before her death, her family and she celebrated the fiftieth anniversary of her marriage to Romualdo Pacheco. Mrs. Pacheco's funeral was held at St. Luke's Catholic Church in San Francisco, California. Mrs. Pacheco was buried in Mountain View Cemetery, Oakland, California, alongside her husband and son.

First Lady Amelia Irwin
Courtesy of California State Library

First Lady Amelia Cassidy Irwin
1875-1880

THIRTEENTH GOVERNOR, WILLIAM IRWIN

It is unfortunate that very little is known about Amelia Elizabeth Cassidy. She was born in England about 1837. The date Amelia Cassidy arrived in California is unknown. When she met William Irwin, she was living in Fort Jones, a military post, with her mother, Mrs. Sterling, who had remarried. Amelia married William Irwin on December 21, 1865, in Yreka, with the Reverend Isaac Reynolds conducting the ceremony.

William, who was the publisher of the Yreka Union, and Amelia Irwin lived in Yreka, Siskiyou County. They had one daughter, Emma, who graduated from Mills College in Oakland in 1885.

William Irwin and Amelia moved to Sacramento when he was elected to the Senate in 1869. When Romualdo Pacheco became governor, William Irwin became lieutenant governor and then governor in 1875. The inaugural ball that was held on December 9, 1875, was one of the most lavish and expensive balls ever held. Although the attendance was unknown, it probably had a large turnout. Mrs. Governor Irwin was described,

"From the shadows of curtained halls of state, one fancies he sees a mannequin of the present. A gracefully gowned figure, in silk, bodice cut low, with an overskirt of illusion atop a silk foundation, and with flowers trimming the costume, passes by. Her hair (the tell-mark of her generation) is in chatelaine braids and curls. She is the wife of the Governor of California—the first lady at the ball."[15]

During Governor Irwin's term, President Grant and Mrs. Grant visited California, and Mrs. Irwin poured tea for Mrs. Grant in the Senate chambers.

William Irwin died in San Francisco on March 15, 1886, and was buried in the City Cemetery of Sacramento. As a result of heart disease, Mrs. Irwin died in Berkeley on October 20, 1905, and was buried at Cypress Lawn Cemetery.

First Lady Ruth Perkins
Courtesy of Butte County Historical Society

First Lady Ruth Parker Perkins
1880-1883

FOURTEENTH GOVERNOR, GEORGE PERKINS

When Ruth Parker was eight years old, her parents and she moved to Marysville, California. She was born in County Cork, Ireland, on August 21, 1843. Her father was Edward Parker, an English officer. Shortly after their arrival, Edward Parker and George Perkins started the firm of Parker and Perkins, the beginning of one of the most extensive business enterprises north of San Francisco, California. Ruth Parker, a beautiful lady, four years younger, and George Perkins were married in Marysville, California, on May 3, 1864. They lived in Oroville, California, for several years, where the Perkins' interests were in mines and the grocery business. George and Ruth Perkins had four children while living in Oroville: Fannie, George, Susan, and Fred. In 1879, George transferred his Oroville interests to his brother; and the family moved to Oakland, California. There, they became the parents of three more children: Milton, Ruth, and Grace. They lived in several large Victorian houses; and in 1893, they built a twenty-two-room Queen Anne mansion, called Palm Knoll. It had a large arboretum so Ruth could enjoy her hobby of growing flowers all year.

As wife of the governor, Mrs. Perkins was fully prepared for the demands of the social functions and carried herself with dignity and grace, which won her many friends. Mrs. Perkins was devoted to her husband and her large family. Mrs. Perkins was also a great student, writing poetry published in magazines and newspapers. She was progressive in her views and writing style.

In July, 1880, five-year-old Milton escaped a serious accident. He poured a quantity of coal oil on the sidewalk to kill some ants. He then lit a kerosene lantern which burst into flames. He was burned around the face and hands. An older brother put out the fire.

Mrs. Perkins was seventy-eight years old when she passed away on February 4, 1921, in Alameda, California. Her death was unexpected, caused by a heart attack. She was buried in Mountain View Cemetery, Oakland, California.

First Lady Mary Stoneman
Courtesy of *Morning Call*, San Francisco, 1891

The Stoneman Ranch
Courtesy of California State Library

First Lady Mary Hardisty Stoneman
1883-1887

FIFTEENTH GOVERNOR, GEORGE STONEMAN

Mary Oliver Hardisty, from a socially prominent family in Baltimore, was born about 1828. The family considered themselves Southerners, being members of the "Reliance Club," which requires being born in the South as a qualification to belong. It is interesting that Mary married George Stoneman, a military man who had graduated from West Point and was a Union officer in the Civil War. While he was still serving in the Civil War, George and Mary were married on November 21, 1861. Mary liked to refer to George as "Stony".

In 1871, the family moved to the San Gabriel Valley in California and settled on a four hundred-acre estate called Las Robles (The Oaks). They had four children: Cornelius; George Jr., who later became a prominent attorney; Katherine Cheney; and Adele.

When George was campaigning to be governor, George traveled up and down the state. It was said that Mary hated campaigning and did not want her husband to be in politics.

As first lady, Mary became very active socially, not only in Sacramento society but San Francisco society as well. She was described as a lady who always wore her eyeglasses and was elegantly dressed. She was known for having a good time and being a very good dancer. It was also said that she did speak her mind and would not be timid about expressing her opinions.

On July 17, 1885, a fire destroyed the Stonemans' ranch home. Mary was brokenhearted, not only because all the family possessions were lost but she discovered George had not paid the insurance, and there would be no help financially.

George and Mary separated. He left California and stayed with his sister in Albany, New York. Later, he traveled to visit another sister in New York state and died there on September 5, 1894.

Mary moved to be with her daughter Katherine in Brookline, Massachusetts, and died in Brookline in 1908.

First Lady Jane Waterman
Courtesy of California State Library

Long Waterman Mansion
Courtesy of Artistic Illuminations, Mark Mullen, San Diego

MENU

SOUP.

PALE GORDON, DUFF SHERRY.

Bouillion with Poached Eggs.   Chicken Gumbo.

HORS D'OEUVRES D'OFFICE.

SAUTERNE, HOC KEIMER—1848.

Eastern Oysters on Half Shell.   Butter.   Sardines in Oil.

Pickles.   California Olives.

FISH

CLARET—ZINFANDEL.

Baked Mountain Trout, a la Maitre d'Hotel.

Mashed Potatoes.

ENTREES.

Broiled Spring Chicken with Breakfast Bacon.   Broiled Quail.

Breaded Sweet Breads with Champignons.

Potatoes a la Jardinere.

ROASTS.

Turkey, Stuffed with Oysters.   Ham, Champagne Sauce.

Chicken.

VEGETABLES.

French Green Peas.   Asparagus.

French Baked Potatoes.

SALADS.

Fresh Crab, Mayonaise Dressing.

Lettuce.   Celery.   Lobster.

COLD DISHES.

Buffalo Tongue.   Eastern Ham.   Eastern Bologna.

Herring.   Shaved Dried Beef.   Venison.

Pressed Corned Beef.

DESSERT.

CHAMPAGNE—ECLIPSE EXTRA DRY.

Meringue Shells filled with Charlotte de Russe.

Champagne Jelly.

ICE CREAM—Strawberry, Pineapple.

Fruit Cake.   Pound Cake.   Citron Cake.   Jelly Cake.

White and Nut Cake.   Maccaroons.   Candy Pyramids.

FRUIT.

Bananas.   Oranges.   Pineapples.   Apples.

Raisins.   Peaches.

PYRAMIDS.

Nuts and Candies.   Ale, Porter and Seltzer.   Black Coffee.

Chartreuse.

FROMAGE.

Swiss.   Cream Amber.   Neuchatel.   Roquefort.

Brie.

Waterman Special Dinner Menu
Courtesy of California State Library

First Lady Jane Gardner Waterman
1887-1891

SEVENTEENTH GOVERNOR, ROBERT W. WATERMAN

Jane Gardner Waterman was born on November 8, 1829, in Stanstead, Lower Canada. It was uncertain when her family moved to Belvidere, Illinois. There were letters to Jane regarding her family who lived in this city. Jane was sent to boarding school in Chicago. On September 29, 1847, when Jane was eighteen, she married Robert Whitney Waterman. At this time, Robert owned a store in Illinois, where he started as a clerk in 1839. The couple had six children: Anna, Waldo, James Sears, Helen Jane, Abby Louisa, and Mary.

In 1851, Robert started overland for California, where he did some mining, and returned home in 1852. In August of 1874, he moved the family, including Jane's sister Charlotte, to a ranch near San Bernardino. From 1880 to 1886, Waterman was busy developing gold and silver mines near Barstow. In 1886, he took possession of the Stonewall Mine in San Diego. That same year, August 11, Jane was sent to a sanitorium in Pennsylvania where she was treated for chronic ailments and nervous exhaustion. The following year, Jane's health improved.

Jane, as first lady, was busy with charities, donations, and many request letters, some asking to influence her husband concerning pardons. When Jane wrote a letter to John Hopkins Medical School about admitting women, they replied that because of the high standards, women could not be admitted; but an endowment of $100,000 might influence the decision. One daughter and one son became physicians.

In 1891, after Governor Waterman's two terms were completed, the family moved to San Diego. For $17,000, they purchased a Queen Anne mansion built by the same craftsman who built the Hotel Del Coronado.

Robert Waterman died on April 12, 1891. Minnie Johnson, Hiram Johnson's wife, wrote a letter of condolence, mentioning plans to have visited them and how she associated all her childhood memories with them. Robert was buried at Mount Hope Cemetery in San Diego.

Jane Waterman died on April 12, 1914, in Barstow, California.

First Lady Mary Markham
Courtesy of California State Library

First Lady Mary Dana Markham
1891-1895

EIGHTEENTH GOVERNOR, HENRY MARKHAM

Although of New England ancestry, Mary Adams Dana was born in Wyoming, Illinois, on July 4, 1853. She was the daughter of Giles Dana of Montpelier, Vermont. Her family moved to Wisconsin, where she spent her childhood years. She was educated in Rockford Seminary, Illinois. Henry Markham married Mary Adams Dana on May 17, 1876, in Waukesha, Wisconsin. The war days had caused a severe strain on Henry Markham's health, and the Markhams decided to move to California. They arrived in Pasadena, California, in 1879 and were among the first pioneer families. They purchased a ranch, bounded by California and Bellefontaine Streets, Fair Oaks and St. John Avenues. The lovely surrounding made it one of the most desirable homes in Pasadena. The Markhams became the parents of five daughters: Marie, Alice, Gertrude, Genevieve, and Hildreth.

Mrs. Markham was a graceful tall lady. While in Pasadena, she became interested in the Congregational Church, now the Neighborhood Church. She was a tireless worker for its causes. She was interested in her husband's causes and always thoughtful toward others.

Henry Markham was elected governor in 1891. For the inauguration ball, Mrs. Markham wore a pale blue empire princess satin brocade gown with a court train. The bodice was trimmed with pearls and blue ostrich tips. She wore blue slippers and carried a blue fan. For a reception in April, 1891, Mrs. Markham wore a seafoam satin gown. The front was trimmed in silver and crystal with a large satin bow. The bodice and skirt of the gown featured light blue feather tips. She wore gloves of the same color, lovely diamonds, and carried a white feather fan.

After six months in office, their daughter Genevieve contracted typhoid fever and died. Mrs. Markham and the four daughters returned to Pasadena, California, to live. For the next three and half years, Mrs. Markham made frequent trips to Sacramento to visit her husband.

After an illness of several months, Mrs. Markham passed away in the family home on May 31, 1934. She was eighty-one years old. She was buried in Mountain View Cemetery in Altadena, California.

First Lady Inez Budd
Courtesy of Haggin Museum, Stockton

GOVERNOR AND MRS. BUDD
As they were sketched at the inaugural ball in his honor,
January 28, 1895, in the capitol.

Governor and Mrs. Budd, Inaugural Ball, 1895
Courtesy of *Sacramento Union*

First Lady Inez Merrill Budd
1895–1899

NINETEENTH GOVERNOR, JAMES BUDD

When Inez A. Merrill was five years old, her family moved to Stockton, California. Inez was born near Hartford, Connecticut, on August 2, 1851. Her parents, both prominent socially, were Marus H. of Connecticut and Celinda A. Clough of Massachusetts.

A romance began between James "Jim" Budd and Inez when they attended the same schools in Stockton. James's father, the Honorable Joseph H. Budd, was one of the city's successful attorneys.

In 1873, Inez married James H. Budd in Stockton. "In every respect, Mrs. Budd was fitted to be the wife of a man of genius and brilliant mind."[16]

Inez and Jim moved to a handsome Victorian mansion in Stockton. Socially, Mr. and Mrs. Budd were well known in California. They had no children.

It must have been difficult for Inez when there was the scandal about James who was charged with betraying his ward Nancy and forging her will. Despite this scandal, James Budd was elected governor.

At the inaugural ball on January 28, 1895, Inez wore "a magnificent garment of white duchesse satin, en trained. Her corsage was *décolleté* with very bouffant sleeves and decorated with pearl trimming and lace. She carried a bouquet of white rosebuds, her hair worn high with diamond ornaments."[17]

Upon retiring from office, Governor Budd moved his law practice to San Francisco. In 1907, James Budd traveled to Europe hoping to find a cure for his failing health. In the spring of 1908, he returned to Stockton, where he maintained a main law office and a branch in San Francisco. He died in Stockton on July 30, 1908. A year later, Inez had an unusual monument at his gravesite—a broken dome supported by three tall granite pillars.[18]

Three or four days before Inez's death, she founded a new religious sect known as the Christ Doctrine Revealed and Astronomical Sciences Association. The association was designated as a religious, scientific, and social organization. The headquarters was at the home of Mrs. Budd, at 1239 East Channel Street, Stockton.

After a brief illness, Inez died on May 15, 1911, and was buried in the Stockton Rural Cemetery.

MRS. HENRY T. GAGE.

First Lady Francisca Gage
Courtesy of A.K. Smiley Library

First Lady Francisca "Fannie" Victoria Rains Gage
1899–1903

TWENTIETH GOVERNOR, HENRY GAGE

In November, 1862, John and Maria Rains, Francisca's parents, signed a mortgage on property in Rancho Cucamonga, California. Two days later, John Rains left his wife and four children in Cucamonga and drove off in a wagon. Eleven days later, he was found murdered. His daughter Francisca Victoria Rains was born on August 3, 1863. The first school in Cucamonga is said to have been started by Maria Rains for her children in 1870.

Francisca Victoria Rains married a young lawyer named Henry T. Gage. The marriage license was dated July 15, 1880, and stated that Henry Gage was a native of New York, age twenty-seven, and Francisca, Fannie, was seventeen.

On September 30, 1880, two months after their marriage, Henry and Fannie Gage purchased an old adobe house on twenty-seven acres in Downey, California. Henry and Fannie Gage had three boys and three girls. All of their children—Arthur, Henry, Volney, Frances, Lucille, and Fanita—were born in the family ranch home.

Henry T. Gage was inaugurated as California's twentieth governor on January 6, 1899. For the inauguration, Mrs. Gage wore a lovely gown, pinched at the waist, with puffed sleeves, and a hat trimmed with ostrich feathers. She was one of the finest-looking women at the ball. As

California's first lady, Fannie Rains Gage welcomed President and Mrs. William McKinley. Governor and Mrs. Gage traveled by train to Redlands, California, in May, 1901, to greet the presidential party. Mrs. Gage also met many of the crowned heads of Europe.

After completing his four-year term, Governor Gage returned to his private law practice. In 1909, President Taft appointed Henry Gage minister to Portugal. However, because of Fannie's ill health, he resigned the position in 1911.

On "Pioneer Day" on August 4, 1946, Fannie Gage returned to visit the home where she was baptized. She recalled when she lived in the house, there were wonderful hot biscuits being baked and served. Fannie Rains Gage died in 1951.

First Lady Helen Pardee
Courtesy of California State Parks, Governor's Mansion SHP, 2006

Governor and Mrs. Pardee
Courtesy of Pardee Mansion, Oakland

Mrs. Pardee and daughters
Courtesy of Pardee Mansion, Oakland

First Lady Helen Penniman Pardee
1903-1907

TWENTY-FIRST GOVERNOR, GEORGE PARDEE

Helen Newman Penniman was a free thinker and an individualist. On July 18, 1857, Helen was born into a Chelsea, Massachusetts, family who could trace their ancestors back to the Revolutionary War. The family moved to San Francisco, and then to Oakland in 1862. Helen, or "Nellie" as she was called, was about eleven years old. Surprisingly, George Pardee moved to Oakland when he was about the same age.

Helen grew up going on camping trips with her friends who called themselves "the Merry Tramps of Oakland," a local bohemian group from middle class families who were interested in hiking, art, and photography. In 1884, Helen, with the Merry Tramps, started a quilt which included a swatch of fabric from one of Mary Todd Lincoln's dresses. These friends called Helen "Blazes", referring to her beautiful red hair and flamboyant personality.

Helen Penniman and George Pardee were high school sweethearts, both attending Oakland High School, and graduated with seventeen other classmates in 1875. Helen and George were married on January 25, 1887. After graduating from the University of California at Berkeley, George Pardee, like his father, became an eye doctor and a mayor of Oakland. Helen attended California State Normal School and taught at the Grove Street School in Oakland for ten years.

The Pardee mansion was built for George's father in 1869. Later, it was home to three generations, and Helen, being an avid collector, made the house into a living museum. She was also an artist, taking art lessons from the artist Yelland. The family had four daughters: Florence, Madeline, Carol, and Helen.

The Pardees were the first family to move into the Governor's Mansion. Helen brought some of her collections to the mansion. As first lady, Helen loved to entertain, and this popular family had many friends and visitors. On one occasion, the Pardees fed the entire University of California Glee Club.

After Governor Pardee's term was completed, the family moved back to their home in Oakland. Helen actively brought the world into her home, continuing to add to her interesting collections from around the world.

Helen Pardee was eighty-nine when she died on March 10, 1947, and was buried with her husband and children in the Mountain View Cemetery in Oakland.

First Lady Isabella Gillette
Courtesy of California State Parks, Governor's Mansion SHP, 2006

First Lady Isabella Erzgraber Gillette
1907-1911

TWENTY-SECOND GOVERNOR, JAMES NORRIS GILLETTE

On May 8, 1898, Isabella Erzgraber, a San Francisco belle, married State Senator James Gillette, a widower with three children. In a letter to Isabella before their marriage, James states: "You will never regret our marriage for I will let no care or sorrow come near you and you will not be unhappy for my whole aim will be your happiness and to keep your love."[19]

Born in 1868, Mrs. Gillette was forty years old when she became California's first lady. She was a talented pianist, and she composed music and wrote poetry. Her book of poetry, *Gleanings and Weavings*, contains forty-seven poems, including this excerpt from *California*:

"By the waves of the blue Pacific, O'verlooking the waters wide, She lies in her beauty majestic, Fair—by the ocean's side, The ocean comes to her door, It enters the Golden Gate, It laps and leaps on her shore, California—our Golden State."[20]

James Norris Gillette Jr. was born in 1901. Mrs. Gillette was constantly fearful for her son's health and safety. She worried that her son would be kidnapped. On May 6, 1909, J. B. Clifton, a San Quentin prisoner, nearly succeeded in kidnapping eight-year-old James Jr., and having the governor grant him freedom as ransom for their son. Governor and Mrs. Gillette were more than pleased when Warden Hoyle discovered the plot and prevented the kidnapping.

Mrs. Gillette was one of the most popular women in the state. Yet, she and her husband led a simple life in the Governor's Mansion in Sacramento. They were happiest with James Jr., their close friends, and their books.

Mrs. Gillette passed away on November 24, 1946, at the age of seventy-nine. She resided in Berkeley, California, and was brought to Sacramento by her son a few weeks before her death. She was buried in Cypress lawn Cemetery in Colma, California. James Gillette Jr. was her only survivor.

Baby Photo of Minnie L. McNeal
Courtesy of California State Library

First Lady Minnie Johnson
Courtesy of California State Parks, Governor's Mansion SHP, 2006

First Lady Minnie L. McNeal Johnson
1911-1917

TWENTY-THIRD GOVERNOR, HIRAM JOHNSON

Minnie L. McNeal and Hiram Johnson were both Sacramento natives: Minnie, born June 11, 1869, and Hiram, September 2, 1866. When Minnie was attending Mills College in Oakland, she met Hiram Johnson, who was a student at the University of California-Berkeley. They were married in 1886, when Hiram was twenty and Minnie was seventeen. They moved back to Sacramento to a house on Seventh and N Streets that Minnie's father had built.

As a result of Minnie's mother's death in childbirth, Minnie was raised by her father who was a well-to-do contractor. According to Frank Snook, a close friend of the Johnsons, Minnie was a very pretty little girl who was full of life and had the liveliest parties in town.[21]

It was said that Minnie did not like Sacramento and soon after their marriage, the couple returned to San Francisco. They had two sons: Hiram Jr. and Archibald.

In 1911, when Hiram was inaugurated as governor, the family returned to Sacramento. Although Mrs. Johnson was small, she had a forceful personality, and was known as "The Boss"[22] by her husband and friends. Because bats were occupying the Governor's Mansion, the family went to live in a hotel for a month. Minnie went to work in making the mansion livable. She had pest eradicators, interior decorators from Gump's in San Francisco, and the entire house renovated. Theodore Roosevelt, former president, visited so many times that the third floor bedroom was called the "Teddy Room."

Minnie was devoted to her family, active socially, and was one of the most successful hostesses. She was said to encourage her husband's political career and was very happy when Hiram became senator in 1917. Minnie was a constant companion to her husband and did not return to San Francisco until the death of Hiram Johnson in 1945.

Minnie McNeal Johnson died on January 25, 1955, at the age of eighty-five. She was survived by a son, Hiram Johnson Jr., a San Francisco attorney. Her other son Archibald had died in 1933.

First Lady Flora Stephens
Courtesy of California State Parks, Governor's Mansion SHP, 2006

First Lady Flora Rawson Stephens
1917-1923

TWENTY-FOURTH GOVERNOR, WILLIAM DENNISON STEPHENS

Flora Rawson was the daughter of Abel Rawson and Lucy Rozier Rawson. She was born on May 16, 1869, in Chicago, Illinois. When she was seven years old, the family moved to California. She finished her education and taught school in Poway, California.

William Denninson Stephens and Flora Rawson were married on June 17, 1891, in San Diego County. They were the parents of one daughter, Barbara.

When Governor Hiram Johnson resigned to enter the United States Congress, William Stephen, the lieutenant governor, succeeded into office. He was governor of California during the anxious years of World War I. Mrs. Stephens was forty-eight years old when she became first lady of California. Although Mrs. Stephens was well educated and filled the position of first lady with dignity and grace, she was never well and some events in the Governor's Mansion were very upsetting. On December 17, 1917, the kitchen and basement laundry rooms were blasted with dynamite. Repairs were made, and the guilty members of the I.W.W. were sent to jail. On February 8, 1922, the cupola of the mansion was struck by a bolt of lightning. The small fire was quickly extinguished.

In 1918, Major Randolph T. Zane, their son-in-law, was killed in action in France. Their daughter, Barbara Zane, and granddaughter, Marjorie, came to live in the Governor's Mansion. On April 21, 1921, Governor and

Mrs. Stephens hosted the first wedding of a governor's daughter in the mansion. Barbara Zane married Dr. John Osburn.

Mrs. Stephens was a life member of the Friday Morning Club of Los Angeles and a member of the Episcopal Church.

Mrs. Stephens passed away on April 21, 1931, in Los Angeles, California, at the age of sixty-two. She had been ill for several years.

First Lady Augusta Richardson
Courtesy of California State Parks, Governor's Mansion SHP, 2006

First Lady Augusta Fielder Richardson
1923-1927

TWENTY-FIFTH GOVERNOR, FRIEND RICHARDSON

When Augusta Fielder was sixteen years old, her family moved from Highland, Illinois, to California, settling in San Bernardino. She was born in 1869, a daughter of a prominent Swiss physician. In San Bernardino on July 23, 1891, Augusta Fielder married Friend Richardson, a Quaker. He was a publisher and the owner of the newspaper *The Times Index*. He enjoyed telling jokes on himself, and it was said that he had visited every town and slept in every hotel in California.

Augusta and Friend Richardson had three children: Ruth, Paul William, and John.

Around 1900, the couple moved to Berkeley, where Friend purchased the *Berkeley Daily Gazette* and was active in the California Press Association. Although Mrs. Richardson did not write articles, she was involved in newspaper circles, and she attended every convention of the California Press Association for forty years.

When Mr. Richardson was appointed state printer, the Richardson family moved to Sacramento. After being elected state treasurer for two terms, Friend Richardson was elected governor in 1923. The family moved to the Governor's Mansion, where "Ma," as Friend called her, was "a crank for cleanliness,"[23] and had everyone involved in cleaning—including the three children. Augusta Richardson was known as a strong and energetic woman, and was the "boss" according to her husband. The collection of first ladies pictures at the mansion shows Mrs. Richardson sitting and crocheting what appears to be a lace tablecloth.

At the end of Governor Richardson's term of office, Augusta and their son John took a year off to travel around the world. In 1941, the Richardsons celebrated their fiftieth wedding anniversary. At the party, one of the speeches to the couple said, "And so the Governor and Ma Richardson go into the afternoon of life, plain people, fine citizens, and upstanding Americans, . . ."[24]

Friend died on September 6, 1943, in Berkeley; and Augusta died on June 17, 1955, in Orinda, California.

First Lady Lyla Young
Courtesy of California State Parks, Governor's Mansion SHP, 2006

First Lady Lyla Vincent Young
1927-1931

TWENTY-SIXTH GOVERNOR, CLEMENT CALHOUN YOUNG

Lyla Vincent's father was from Iowa; her mother from Ireland. She was born on July 23, 1880, in Alameda, California. Lyla Vincent was a student at Stanford University when she met Clement Calhoun Young. On March 15, 1902, Clement Calhoun Young married Lyla Vincent of San Francisco, California. After the 1906 San Francisco earthquake and fire, they moved from San Francisco to Berkeley, California. They were the parents of two daughters, Barbara and Lucy. Mrs. Young was forty-six years old when she became first lady of California.

Mrs. Young was exquisite, dainty, and charming. She was very fond of their Berkeley home. When C. C. Young became governor, they moved to the Governor's Mansion in Sacramento; she made several changes to the decor. She had the dark red draperies all remade, the halls painted a soft cream color, purchased a long pecan wood sideboard for the entry hall and a richly framed mirror to place over the sideboard. She also added some of the Youngs' personal furnishings: their Oriental rugs placed on the red carpet, lamps, and lampshades. The Youngs were the first family to add a radio in the mansion.

Mrs. Young once again established the custom of Thursday afternoon "At Home" for friends in Sacramento. On March 10, 1927, the Youngs received over two hundred guests at the mansion, including members of the Assembly and Senate, their wives, and family members. Even with all of the changes through the Great Depression, World War I, and the postwar problems, Governor and Mrs. Young were a quiet first family. When the two daughters returned from college, they had many friends visiting at the mansion.

Mrs. Young, following a brief illness, passed away on June 9, 1967, in Berkeley, California. She was eighty-six years old. She was buried at Sunset View Cemetery in Berkeley, California.

First Lady Annie Rolph
Courtesy of California State Parks, Governor's Mansion SHP, 2006

First Lady Annie Reid Rolph
1931-1934

TWENTY-SEVENTH GOVERNOR, JAMES ROLPH

When Annie Rolph became first lady of California, she was already experienced as a political wife, being a mayor's wife in San Francisco for nineteen years. James was known as "Sunny Jim" and never wore shoes, only boots. Annie Marshall Reid was born in San Francisco in 1882. James Rolph was also born in this city in 1869. The two of them grew up as neighbors, attending the same school, Valencia Street School. Their fathers were close friends, so the families were together on many occasions. Annie Reid was Jim's girlfriend, and when they were courting, they would send signals to each other from their homes.

On June 26, 1900, Annie Marshall Reid, age eighteen, married James Rolph Jr., age thirty-one, at the Trinity Presbyterian Church on the corner of Twenty-third and Capp Streets in San Francisco. ". . . In consequence, the church was crowded to the doors, and the universal comment was that a handsomer couple had never been wedded in Trinity."[25] They took a two-month-honeymoon to the Hawaiian Islands.

They had three children: Annette (Mrs. John P. Symes), James, the Third, and Georgiana (Mrs. Richard Willetts). Before the stock market crashed in 1929, the Rolphs entertained lavishly. One such instance was when they chartered a train for one hundred and thirty-four guests and entertained them for three days.

In 1931, when Rolph was elected governor, Annie, now forty-nine, and he moved to Sacramento. They kept their house in San Francisco. Sunny Jim loved to see Annie dress in "Alice Blue" and listen to the song "Smiles."[26] Annie, a petite lady, was an accomplished musician and a very charming hostess, giving teas that were open to the public. Annie Rolph had the crystal chandelier installed in the dining room of the mansion.

In Marysville on February 28, 1934, James Rolph suffered a stroke. While still in office, he died on June 2, 1934.

Annie died on September 23, 1956, in San Francisco.

First Lady Jessie Merriam
Courtesy of California State Parks, Governor's Mansion SHP, 2006

First Lady Jessie Stewart Merriam 1936-1939

TWENTY-EIGHTH GOVERNOR, FRANK MERRIAM

Mrs. Lipsey was the widow of A. M. Lipsey. Jessie Stewart was born on September 5, 1869, in Iowa. The Merriams and Lipseys were close friends in Iowa and later in Long Beach, California. On January 25, 1936, Governor Frank Merriam, a widower, married Jessie Lipsey in Palm Springs, California. They moved into the Governor's Mansion on January 27, 1936.

Mrs. Merriam was a smiling, dignified first lady, with a quick sense of humor. She had blue eyes, dimples, fair skin, and short wavy hair. She stood erect, held her chin high, and walked with a spring in her step. Mrs. Merriam was delighted with her new home, Sacramento, and the residents, who enthusiastically welcomed her.

The Merriams held many delightful functions in the Governor's Mansion and throughout the city. On March 11, 1936, Sacramento women greeted Mrs. Merriam at a reception at the Tuesday Clubhouse given by the Woman's Council. Mrs. Merriam stood for hours to meet more than seven hundred women who came to welcome her. In the spring of 1936, Mrs. Merriam gave a tea at the Governor's Mansion for the wives of the California State Bankers Association. Mrs. Eleanor Roosevelt was honored at a tea given by Mrs. Merriam on March 19, 1938. The first "Woman's Day" was held on September 8, 1938, in Merriam Hall at the then State Fair grounds in Sacramento. Eleven hundred women attended; five hundred had to be turned away. Mrs. Merriam looked at the crowd and said, "Aren't women wonderful?"[27]

Mrs. Merriam shunned publicity about her civic and benevolent activities. She was actively involved in the Day Nursery and Navy Chapel in Long Beach, California, and she was on the Board of Directors of the home for elderly members of the P.E.O. in Alhambra, California. For sixty-two years, she was a member of P.E.O.

Mrs. Merriam passed away on July 13, 1948, in Long Beach, California and was buried in Forest Lawn Cemetery, Long Beach, California.

First Lady Kate Olson
Courtesy of California State Parks, Governor's Mansion SHP, 2006

First Lady Kate Jeremy Olson
January 1939–April 1939

TWENTY-NINTH GOVERNOR, CULBERT OLSON

In 1920, Kate and Culbert Olson moved to Los Angeles, where they lived in the same house for thirty-nine years. Kate Jeremy was born in 1883, growing up in a Mormon family in Utah. Kate was a free thinker, and she didn't take religious beliefs too seriously. In 1905, Kate Jeremy, age twenty-two, married Culbert Olson, age twenty-eight. Olson's mother had been a suffragette, so Kate and Culbert were compatible in their social and religious philosophies. The couple had three children: Richard, and the twins; John and Dean.

Even though Mrs. Olson was ill in Los Angeles, she did attend the inaugural ball held at the Memorial Auditorium on January 6, 1939. A description of her gown was mentioned in the *Sacramento Bee.* ". . . . a majestic black velvet made on simple lines with a sweeping skirt and cut-out three quarter length sleeves. Her flowers will be orchids, and her jewels will be diamonds in a bracelet, and rings."[28] On January 8, at his inauguration, Governor Olson became ill and was hospitalized until February. This made for a difficult move to the mansion, resulting in Mrs. Olson's health becoming worse.

Kate Olson loved to play cards and poker—having been in a poker club in Los Angeles. In the mansion, the game would consist of friends and include security guards, who would play for a half a cent a chip. Sometimes they would play all night, one session lasting until five-thirty in the morning.

One employee remarked that" Mrs. Olson taught her how to play without losing her shirt".[29]

Although Kate had health problems, she still had a sense of humor. When asked about how much influence she thought she had as first lady, she replied, . . ." she liked to think of herself as the powder behind the Keg."[30]

On April 15, 1939, Kate Olson had three cerebral hemorrhages within a few hours and died in the mansion at the age of fifty-six. She was the only first lady to die in the mansion.

When giving her portrait to the mansion, Culbert Olson said, "It makes me very happy to know that this portrait of my lovely Kate will hang forever on the walls of the mansion she could enjoy for so short a time."[31]

First Lady Nina Warren
Courtesy of California State Parks, Governor's Mansion SHP, 2006

Mrs. Warren's Chocolate Cake Recipe

1/4 lb butter
1 C. granulated sugar
1C. brown sugar
3 oz. unsweetened chocolate, melted
6 egg yokes
3 tsp cold water
2 C. cake flour
1 tsp soda dash of salt
1C. buttermilk
1 tsp vanilla

Cream butter and sugars thoroughly; add melted chocolate. Beat egg yokes with water and add to creamed mixture. Sift together 3 times the flour, soda, and salt. Add to creamed mixture, alternately with the buttermilk until all is used. Add vanilla and beat until well mixed. Pour batter into two greased and floured 9-inch cake pans and bake at 350 degrees 35 minutes or until cakes tested done.

Fill between layers with Seven Minute Frosting and frost top and sides with Chocolate Frosting.

Seven Minute frosting

2 egg whites
1 1/2 cups granulated sugar
1 1/2 tsp light corn syrup
5 tbsp cold water
1 tsp vanilla

Place all ingredients except vanilla in the top of a double boilier. Place the pan over boiling water and beat egg white mixture with an electric mixer for 7 minutes or until mixture stands up in peaks. Remove from heat and add vanilla.

Courtesy of the Betty Henderson Collection

First Lady Nina Palmquist Warren
1943-1953

THIRTIETH GOVERNOR, EARL WARREN

Nina Palmquist came to California as an infant with her parents and grew up in Oakland, California. She was born in Gutland, Sweden, on March 9, 1893. Nina Palmquist married Grover Meyers and had a son, James. Grover Meyers died in 1920. In 1925, Mrs. Meyers met Earl Warren at a swimming party. They were married on October 14, 1925. Earl Warren adopted James. The Warrens became the parents of five children: Virginia, Earl Jr., Dorothy, Nina Elisabeth (Honey Bear), and Robert.

When she became California's first lady, Mrs. Warren was overwhelmed with what was needed to be done to make the Governor's Mansion a home. Mrs. Warren commuted from Oakland to Sacramento until she had the Governor's Mansion renovated. She had all the rooms painted, purchased Oriental rugs, converted a screened-in porch into a closed-in bedroom, made two small servant rooms into one bedroom, and made major changes in the kitchen. The Warren family moved into the Governor's Mansion on April 1, 1943.

Mrs. Warren was a beautiful blonde, with a quick smile, a lovely husky voice, and incredible energy. She hosted marvelous teas for the wives of the Legislators and close friends, formal dinner parties, official state functions, informal gatherings for the children, and was the honored guest at many occasions. For family and guests, she enjoyed cooking, particularly chocolate cakes, Swedish dishes, and all the bread. She often cooked meals for needy families, enclosing a note stating they had food left over and would appreciate help in eating it. Even though there was a housekeeper, the Warren children cleaned their own rooms and had a variety of odd jobs to earn extra money.

The Warrens were the longest occupants of the Governor's Mansion. They had lived there ten years when, on October 4, 1953, President Eisenhower appointed Governor Warren Chief Justice of the United States. Mrs. Warren packed and moved ten years of personal effects for all seven family members. On December 7, 1953, Mrs. Warren moved to Washington, D.C.

Mrs. Warren passed away on April 24, 1993. She was one hundred years old. She was buried at Arlington National Cemetery next to her husband.

First Lady Virginia Knight
Courtesy of California State Parks, Governor's Mansion SHP, 2006

First Lady Virginia Carlson Knight
1954-1959

THIRTY-FIRST GOVERNOR, GOODWIN KNIGHT

Virginia Francis Carlson Knight was not only the youngest first lady to live in the Governor's Mansion, but was also one of the most admired women of her time. Not only was she beautiful and charming, she was also a talented poet, receiving many awards for her work. She received the Certificate of Merit from the World of Who's Who of Women, as well as recognition of Who's Who in California.

Virginia Francis Piergue was born on October 12, 1918, in Fort Dodge, Iowa. Her family moved to Los Angeles in 1923, where Virginia attended Alta Loma Grammar School. She graduated from Los Angeles High School in 1937, and married Lieutenant C. Lyle Carlson on June 28, 1940. In 1944, Lieutenant Carlson was shot down over Italy, and Virginia Carlson became a widow. She devoted a lot of her time visiting veterans. The Purple Heart organization named her as "Viola Queen."

When Virginia first met Lieutenant Governor Goodwin Knight, she was working on a television show, *Freedom Forum.* Before Governor Knight's first term of office, his wife had died. Three months before his reelection of his second term on August 16, 1954, Governor Goodwin Knight married Virginia Carlson.

The press loved Virginia and the idea of the romance between the governor and her. Being a former model and selected for the ten best-dressed women, Virginia's clothes were described in many newspaper articles.

When she was carried over the threshold at the Governor's Mansion, she gasped. "It is a palace. I felt like Cinderella when I saw my new home for the first time."[32] Virginia loved the mansion; remodeling many rooms; her favorite room being the Scandinavian kitchen.

She became interested in the former first ladies and started a project that researched all the first ladies that lived in the mansion. "I feel sure that some day this beautiful home will become a museum," she prophesized, "and I think people will be interested in the women who have lived here."[33]

Goodwin Knight died in Inglewood, on May 22, 1970, and was buried in Rose Hills Memorial Park. Virginia Knight lives in Los Angeles.

First Lady Bernice Brown
Courtesy of California State Parks, Governor's Mansion SHP, 2006

First Lady Bernice Layne Brown
1959-1967

THIRTY-SECOND GOVERNOR, EDMUND "PAT" G. BROWN

Bernice Layne was the daughter of Police Captain Arthur Layne and Alice Cuneo. She was born in San Francisco, California, on November 19, 1908. For her early schooling Bernice attended an experimental program where students worked at their own pace. Bermice's accelerated pace allowed her to graduate from elementary school at age ten and Lowell High School in San Francisco at age fourteen. She met Edmund Brown at Lowell High School when she was a junior and he was a senior. She graduated from the University of California-Berkeley, studied a fifth year; and received her teaching credential. They eloped to Reno, Nevada, on October 30, 1930. They were the parents of four children: Barbara, Cynthia, Edmund "Jerry" G. Jr., and Kathleen.

Mrs. Brown was ambivalent about politics. She was proper, restrained, and known as the disciplinarian at home. On June 3, 1960, a press release from the governor's office emphasized, "Mrs. Brown frankly admits she never would have chosen a political career for her husband if the choice had been hers to make."[34] She gracefully assumed the role of a politician's wife and supported her husband throughout his career.

Mrs. Brown was interested in California history. She borrowed works of art from California museums to use in the Governor's Mansion. She continued the public tours of the Governor's Mansion begun by Mrs. Knight. As first lady, she was a much-sought-after speaker. Her talks were on experiences as a governor's wife and life in the Governor's Mansion. On March 12, 1959, Mrs. Brown hosted the San Francisco League of Women Voters at the Governor's Mansion. In May, 1963, the Browns held a dinner reception at the Governor's Mansion for 160 consuls general and their wives. Mrs. Brown was also instrumental in getting a swimming pool on the mansion grounds. In July 1959, a swimming pool was installed as a gift of "Friends of Pat Brown." No contribution was larger than fifty dollars.[35] Mrs. Brown was an avid golfer, accumulating many trophies and awards. On election days when Pat was a candidate, they always played golf after voting. One of her fond memories in the Governor's Mansion was the Christmas she had to keep three bicycles hidden from her curious children.

Mrs. Brown's health declined until she was blind and bedridden. She passed away on May 9, 2002, at the age of ninety-three. She was buried at Holy Cross Cemetery in San Mateo, California.

Nancy Davis, Age 5,
Courtesy of the Ronald Reagan Presidential Foundation and Library

First Lady Nancy Reagan
Courtesy of California State Parks, Governor's Mansion SHP, 2006

Courtesy of the Ronald Reagan Presidential Foundation and Library

First Lady Nancy Davis Reagan
1967–1975

THIRTY-THIRD GOVERNOR, RONALD REAGAN

Nancy Davis Reagan was another first lady that had a legendary romance with her husband that lasted for fifty-two years. She said, "My life began when I married my husband."[36] That marriage with Ronald Reagan took place in Los Angeles, on March 4, 1952.

Anne Francis Robbins, Nancy Davis, was born on July 6, 1921, in New York City. When she was six years old, her mother, an actress, married Dr. Loyal Davis, who later adopted Nancy, an only child. The family moved to Chicago where Nancy attended Girls' Latin School. Nancy graduated from Smith College with a major in theater. She performed in eleven films, her last film playing opposite Ronald Reagan in "Hellcats of the Navy." They had met in 1951, when Ronald Reagan was the president of the Screen Actors Guild.

Nancy wanted to be a wife and felt "a woman's real happiness and fulfillment come from within the home with her husband and children."[37] The couple had two children: Patricia Ann, "Patti," born March 5, 1953; and Ronald Prescott, "Skipper," born on May 20, 1958. Not only was Mrs. Reagan busy with the family, she spent many hours working with many different charities.

In January, 1967, Ronald Reagan became governor, and the family moved into the Governor's Mansion for four months. Nancy, fearing for the safety of her children, decided to move the family out of the mansion to 1341 Forty-fifth Street.

Much to the delight of the photographers, Nancy Reagan was glamorous, very stylish, and youthful. The Reagans' loving relationship was apparent to all who came in contact with them. An example is this letter written to Nancy:

"There are no words to describe the happiness you have brought to the governor. It is no secret that he is the most married man in the world and would be totally lost and desolate without you. Your in luv Guv."[38]

Nancy Reagan was a graceful hostess and an active first lady—attending many fundraisers; visiting veterans, the elderly, the handicapped; and supporting the Foster Grandparent Program. She wrote three books: *To Love a Child*, *My Turn*, and *I Love You, Ronnie*. As first lady of the United States, she went on to fight drug and alcohol abuse among young people.

Mrs. Reagan spent the last ten years caring for Ronald Reagan who had Alzheimer's disease. He died on June 5, 2004. Nancy Reagan lives in the Los Angeles area, is a strong supporter of stem cell research, and works with the Ronald Reagan Library.

First Lady Gloria Deukmejian
Courtesy of Gloria Deukmejian

First Lady Gloria Saatjian Deukmejian 1983-1991

THIRTY-FIFTH GOVERNOR, GEORGE DEUKMEJIAN

After a six-month courtship, Gloria M. Saatjian married George "Duke" Deukmejian on February 16, 1957. Gloria was born in Long Beach in 1933. Both George and Gloria were of Armenian heritage and children of immigrants.

In 1963, George was elected to the State Assembly. For the next twenty-two years, the family rented houses or apartments in Sacramento, while maintaining their home in Southern California.

In Long Beach, Gloria was busy with three children: Leslie, born in 1964; George Jr. in 1966; and Andrea in 1969. She was actively involved in the community with volunteer activities as public school volunteer, PTA, Girl Scouts, Bluebirds-Campfire, Jonathan Jacques Children's Cancer Center, St. Mary's Hospital volunteer, Assistance League of Long Beach and Sacramento, and Long Beach Day Nursery Board.

George became governor in 1983, and Gloria continued being active in her volunteer work in many different organizations.

As first lady, Gloria was:

"Instrumental in developing a statewide awards program to recognize outstanding volunteer achievement for Volunteer Centers of California. Non-Profit charitable organizations could not function without the commitment of volunteers. I am proud of the alliance of Volunteer Centers of California which has enabled concerned citizens to give of their time and talents to help persons in need of assistance. Each year, a "Founders Award" is given in Gloria Deukmejian's name."*

Although Gloria was an experienced wife of a politician, she still had to make many sacrifices. There was little privacy, few vacations, and last-minute changes. This affectionate couple managed to maintain a good relationship, which George credited to Gloria who kept them together with her patience and sense of humor.

After George's term of office was completed, George and Gloria returned to their home in Long Beach, where they continue to be busy with many service projects in their community; co-chairing the Stepping Stones Scholarship Campaign, which helps financially underprivileged children to attend the Long Beach Day Nursery; and supporting the California State University Long Beach Disabled Student Services. Gloria serves on St. Mary Hospital Board of Trustees and Rancho Los Alamitos Foundation Board. Presently, George and Gloria have five grandchildren.

*   Courtesy of Gloria Deukmejian

Governor and Mrs. Pete Wilson
Courtesy of Mrs. Gayle Wilson

First Lady Gayle Edlund Wilson
1991-1999

THIRTY-SIXTH GOVERNOR, PETE WILSON

Gayle Wilson has often been described as a "career volunteer" and a woman dedicated to helping others help themselves. Gayle Edlund was born in Phoenix, Arizona, the middle child of Clarence and Charlotte Edlund. As a high school senior she achieved academic recognition as valedictorian of her class as well as being named one of the forty finalists in the national Westinghouse Science Talent Search. She was also named "Most Outstanding Girl Student" nationally, by the BPOE Elks USA. Gayle continued her education at Stanford University, where she earned her Phi Beta Kappa key and a degree in biology.

Following marriage and graduation, she moved to San Diego, California, to raise her two sons; Todd and Philip Graham. She became involved in a variety of volunteer activities, including being President of the Junior League of San Diego.

Gayle and Pete Wilson met at a political event in the early 1960s, but their romance didn't blossom until she volunteered in his San Diego office during his campaign for United States Senate in 1982. They were married in the Congressional Chapel in the Capitol in Washington, D.C., on May 29, 1983.

As the wife of a United States Senator, Gayle sought to educate herself and Pete about child abuse, drug exposed babies, and issues surrounding early childhood health. She also began her twenty-year service on the board of the Center for Excellence in Education, where she gained the experience of providing educational enrichment and research opportunities for academically talented high school students who excel in math and science.

In 1991, when she and Governor Wilson moved to Sacramento, Gayle Wilson was the first First Lady to establish her office in the state capitol. As first lady, she focused her attention on the dual issues of early childhood health and math/science education. She actively promoted prenatal care, the prevention of drug-exposed babies and abused children, as well as childhood mental health; working to ensure that all of California's children begin their lives healthy, and that they arrive at school ready to learn.

Mrs. Wilson's passion for encouraging and supporting young people who excel in math and science bore fruit in Governor Wilson's last year as governor, when the legislation was passed—and funds appropriated—to create The State Summer School for Math and Science (COSMOS), a four-week residential program for high achieving students, which continues to be hosted on University of California campuses.

In addition to her many other activities, Mrs. Wilson served as the honorary chair, but primary advocate for the restoration of the Leland Stanford Mansion in Sacramento, California, which would be used for official events by the governor and the legislature.

Mrs. Wilson loves to sing and is interested in musical theater. She is also an amateur lyricist. While living in Sacramento, Mrs. Wilson performed each year in the Celebrity Concert, which benefited such charities as the Stanford Home for Children and the Family Service Agency. Mrs. Wilson is also a watercolorist, having studied under Lisa Carpenter in Sacramento.

Gayle and Pete Wilson currently live in Los Angeles, where she is a member of the Board of Directors of Gilead Sciences, Inc., the Caltech Board of Trustees, the Parsons Foundation Board, the Education Financing Foundation of California, and she is chairman of the Advisory Board, and chief fundraiser for COSMOS.

Courtesy of Mrs. Gayle Wilson

First Lady Sharon Davis
Courtesy of Mrs. Sharon Davis

First Lady Sharon Ryer Davis
1999-2003

THIRTY-SEVENTH GOVERNOR, GRAY DAVIS

In 1978, while serving as Chief of Staff to Governor Jerry Brown, Gray Davis arrived late for a flight to Los Angeles. Little did he know he would meet his future wife. Sharon Ryer was a flight attendant working the flight and jokingly chided him for being late. He was taken aback, but he never forgot her. In the course of several months, he saw her four more times on various flights and finally asked her for a date. And thus began a long-distance romance with him in Sacramento, and she in her hometown of San Diego.

Sharon was born in 1954 to Donald and Mary Ryer, the fourth child in a family that grew to seven children. Her father was a Master Chief in the United States Navy, serving in World War II, the Korean War, and Vietnam War, while her mother stayed home to care for her growing brood. In 1963, the family moved to East San Diego County to the small community of Santee.

A shy young girl, who hid behind thick glasses and big sweaters, she once remarked that she did not have bad hair days, but bad hair years. Through her parent's loving support, she came out of her shell and went on to become Miss Santee. While working as a flight attendant, she returned to college at California State University, Sacramento.

In 1983, Sharon and Gray wed and settled into a hectic life in Los Angeles. His election to the State Assembly required weekly commutes to the State Capitol, and she continued to work for the airline and also started a second career in marketing. With her people skills, she took to politics quickly and soon she was dubbed "the rock" by the campaign staff. For the next fifteen years, there were campaigns, Gray's reelection to the Assembly, his two terms as State Controller, and one term as Lieutenant Governor. In 1998, he pulled off a stunning come-from-behind victory and was elected Governor.

As first lady, Sharon focused her attention on children's health, safety and well-being, traveling the state to promote these issues and her husband's education reforms. She wrote a children's book titled, *The Adventures of Capitol Kitty*, a fictional story about a real cat that lived at the Capitol. The proceeds from the book supported her successful efforts to raise funds for school libraries. She was actively involved in the Stanford Mansion project.

After leaving office, the Davises' returned to Los Angeles, where he joined a law firm, and Sharon devotes her time to volunteer efforts on behalf of UNICEF, Loyola Marymount University, and SheVotes.org., a project she started to encourage women to vote.

Courtesy of Mrs. Sharon Davis

First Lady Maria Shriver Schwarzenegger
Courtesy of Maria Shriver

First Lady Maria Shriver Schwarzenegger 2003—

THIRTY-EIGHTH GOVERNOR, ARNOLD SCHWARZENEGGER

Maria Owings Shriver grew up in a prominent political family; her mother being a sister to President John F. Kennedy; and her father being an ambassador and creator of the Peace Corps. Maria was born on November 6, 1955, in Chicago, Illinois. She was the second child, growing up with four brothers. The family philosophy was you can make a difference in life.

She attended Georgetown University where she received a bachelor's degree in American Studies. Maria became an award-winning broadcast journalist as well as a best-selling author. In 1977, at a Kennedy-sponsored event, Maria met Arnold Schwarzenegger, a body builder and actor. Despite their political differences, he being a staunch Republican, they were married on April 26, 1986. Maria had to wear sneakers under her Christian Dior wedding gown because she had two broken toes. Maria teased her uncle, Senator Edward Kennedy, "Don't look at him as a Republican, look at him as the man I love, and if that doesn't work, look at him as someone who can squash you."[39] Maria and Arnold have four children: Katherine Eunice, Christina Maria Aurelia, Patrick Arnold, and Christopher Sargent Shriver.

Although she feels her family comes first, Maria, as first lady, has many roles to fill. She has been an active first lady supporting many programs, such as Military Families Initiative and Heroic Families Program. She is also a supporter of Special Olympics, founded by her mother, and Best Buddies, a one-on-one partnership program for people with disabilities. Maria has continued to encourage women's success. As chair of the California Governors and First Lady's Conference, Maria created the Minerva Award, honoring women for making outstanding contributions to create positive change, and making a difference in the life of Californians. Maria was instrumental in creating the California Museum for History, Women and the Arts. Maria continues to be a supportive wife, mother, and an active first lady.

Bibliography

A.K. Smiley Public Library, Redlands, California.

Allen, Benjamin, *California*, Vol. 2.,(San Francisco: B. S. Allen, 1910).

Alta California, January 12, 1852, November 2, 1863.

Bancroft, Hubert, *History of The Life of Leland Stanford.* (Oakland, California: Biobooks, 1952).

Bancroft Library, University of California, Berkeley, Waterman Family Carton 1-3, Manuscript C-B 491.

Barrows, "Los Angeles County Pioneers of Southern California Reports".

Bissell Mansion Restaurant and Dinner Theater Pamphlet, 4426 Randall Place, St. Louis, Missouri.

Berkeley Daily Gazette, June 18, 1955.

Black, Esther Boulton, *Rancho Cucamonga and Dona Merced.* (Riverside, California: Rubidoux Printing Co., 1975).

Buffalo Courtier, September 6,7,8, 1894.

Butte County Historical Society, P.O. Box 2195, Oroville, California.

California State Library, Bio File: Peter Burnett, John Bigler, John Weller, John Downey, George Stoneman, Goodwin Knight.

California Governor Davis's Inauguration Program, Biography of Sharon Davis.

California Historical Society, 678 Mission Street, San Francisco, California.

California Historical Society Quarterly Journal, Vol. XIX., No. 3. September, 1940.

Conmy, Peter Thomas, *Romauldo Pacheco; Distinguished Californian of the Mexican and American Periods.* (San Francisco: Grand Parlor, Native Sons of the Golden West, 1957).

Connolly, Elaine, Dian Self, *Capital Women.* (Sacramento, California: The Capital Women's History Project, 1995).

Cummins, Ella Sterling, *The Story of the Files.* (San Francisco, California : Worlds Fair Commission of California, 1893).

Cypress Lawn Cemetery, El Camino Real, Coloma, California

Daily Evening Bulletin, January 12, 1860.

Daily Examiner, March 31, 1866.

Daggett Scrapbook, Vol. 3.

Davis, Winfield J., *History of Political Convention in California,* 1848-1892, (Publication of the California State Library).

Detwiler, Justice (Editor), *Who's Who in California, A Biographical Directory,* 1928-1929. (San Francisco: Who's Who Publishing Co., 1929).

Evening Bee, January 10, 1899.

Fletcher, Russell (Editor), *Who's Who in California,* Vol. 1, 1942-1943. (Los Angeles, California: Who's Who Publishing Co., 1943).

Gillette Collection, Archives Library, Incoming Correspondence.

Gillette, Isabella, *Gleanings and Weavings.* (San Francisco: Marvin Cloyd, 1922).

Guinn, J. M., *Historical and Biographical Record of Los Angeles and Vicinity.* (Chicago: Chapman Publishing Company, 1901).

Haggin Museum, Victory Park, 1201 N. Pershing Ave. Stockton, California.

Haiman, Miecislaus, *Polish Pioneers of California.* (Illinois: Polish R. C. Union of America, 1940).

Henderson, Betty, *Families in the Mansion.*(Sacramento, California: Sacramento County Historical Society, 1973).

Hittle, T. H., *History of California,* Vol. 4. (San Francisco: N. J. Stone and Company. 1898).

Interview with David Nicolai, Museum Director, Pardee Mansion, Oakland, California, June 16, 2006.

Internet

www.accessgenealogy.com

www.arnoldschwarzenegger.gov.ca

www.aauwsf.org

www.absoluteastronomy.com

www.capitolmuseum.ca.gov/english/remarkable/panel 5.html

www.citivu.com/re/hist/html

www.downeyca.com

www.en.wikipedia.org

www.geocities.com/npmaling/perkins6.html.
www.gray-davis.com.
www. infoplease.com. /biography/us/congress.
www.investors.gilead.com
www.loc.gov.rr.hispanic/congress/pacheco.html
www.mariashriver.com
www.nationalreview.com.
www.oaklandmemorial,/class of 1875.
www.politicalgraveyard.com
www.placesearth.com/usa/california/san
www.ronaldreaganlibrary.com
www.scvhistory.com
www.sfmuseum.org/hist5/callib.html
www.search.com/reference/john-mcdougal
www.search.com/reference/romauldo-pacheco
www.search.com/reference/illiam-stephens
www.stanfordmuseum.org/then-history.html
www.wic.org/bio/gwilson.html.
www.ucop.edu/cosmos/news/gwilson.html
www.ulwaf.com. www.whitehouse.com/firstladies.

John Rains House, National Register of Historical Places, pamphlet.
Journal of San Diego History, Summer 1982, Vol. 28, No 3.
Latter Day Saints, Multi-Stake House, Family History Center, Sacramento, California.
Lenhoff, James, "From Sailor to Senator". Diggins, Vol. 24, No. 2. (Butte County Historical Society, 1980).
Lewis, Donovan, *Pioneers of California.* (Scottwell Associates, 2nd Ed., November,1993).
Long Beach Day Nursery News, Spring, 2005.
Long Beach Press Telegraph, July 14, 1948.
Lyons, Louis, *Who's Who Among the Women of California.* (San Francisco: Security Publishing Company, 1922).
Martin, Covert, *Stockton Album through the Years.*
Melendy, Brett, Benjamin Gilbert, *The Governors of California From Peter Burnett to Edmund G. Brown.* (California: Talisman Press, 1965).
Melendy, Brett, "Who Was John McDougal", *Pacific Historical Review,* Vol. 29, August, 1960.
Mercer County Historical Society and Museum, Mercer, Pennsylvania.
Mercer County Historical Society, Letter of George R. Bigler, June 29, 1929.
Mercer County Bigler Cemetery, Mercer, Pennsylvania.
Missouri Historical Society, 225 South Skinker Blvd., St. Louis, Missouri.

Missouri State Archives, P.O. Box 1747, 600 West Main, Jefferson City, Missouri.

Morning Appeal, November 26, 1887, November 26, 1887.

Mountain View Cemetery, 5000 Piedmont Ave, Oakland, California.

Mullen, Mark, Artistic Illumination, San Diego, California.

Myers, Sandra (Editor), *Ho for California.* (California: Huntington Library, 1980).

Oakland Times, March 30, 1898.

Oakland Tribune, March 30, 1898, March 11, 1947.

Oroville Daily Register, February 5, 1921.

Overland. (January, 1914, 63:23).

Pasadena Star News, October 9, 1923, May 31, 1934.

Pickett, Barbara, *The Life of John McDougal, The Second Governor of California.* (Sacramento: Senior Seminar Paper, 1939).

Rarick, Ethan, *The Life and Time of Pat Brown, California Rising.* (Berkeley, California: University of California Press, 2005).

Rice, Bertha Marguerite, *The Women of Our Valley. (Bertha M. Rice,*1956), Vol.2.

Sacramento Bee. February 8, 1873, March 15, 1886, January 24, 1891, March 1, 1891, March 7, 1891, March 30, 1898, October 23, 1905, October 2, 1910, February 5, 1921, March 10, 1927, January 7, 1931, April 22, 1931, January 9, 1935, January 25, 1936, January 27, 1936, January 28, 1936, March 12, 1936, March 18, 1938, March 21, 1938, January 6, 1939, April 15, 1939, September 6, 1943, April 26, 1944, August 6, 1945, November 25, 1946, December 4, 1953, December 7, 1953, January 6, 1955, January 25, 1955, July 11, 1955, July 30, 1958, October 22, 1958, December 30, 1962, May 20, 1973, September 30, 1973, October 30, 1977, November 1, 1977, March 5, 1980, October 4, 1984, May 11, 2002.

Sacramento City Cemetery Archives, Sacramento, California.

Sacramento Historical Journal, Vol. IV., No. 4.

Sacramento Magazine, Vol. II, No. 1, January 1985.

Sacramento Union, January 9, 1856, January 11, 1860, January 5,1867, December 17, 1867, September 23, 1871, September 2, 1872, November 17, 1873, August 18, 1875, January 11, 1895, January 18, 1895, March 30, 1898, April 26, 1921, May 2, 1942, January 10, 1943, April 26, 1944, January 4, 1959, May 19, 1985.

San Diego Union, May 19, 1985.

San Francisco Alta, January 26, 1851, June 28, 1851, July 31, 1854, March 10, 1855, May 14, 1855, August 4, 1857, September 18, 1860, May 18, 1873, October 31, 1873, November 1, 1873, September 2, 1875.

San Francisco Call, January 11, 1851, January 12, 1860, February 3, 1863, June 24, 1882, January 29, 1883, July 11, 1883, July 18, 1885, November 24, 1887, May 18, 1890, July 27, 1890, January 10, 1891, March 1, 1891,

April 12,1891, April 18, 1891, June 14, 1891, March 2, 1894, May 18, 1895, June 27, 1900, May 6, 1909.

San Francisco Chronicle, February 7, 1872, December 12, 1897, February 6, 1898, October 2, 1910, November 6, 1913, November 7, 1913, April 28, 1926, January 3, 1934, June 1, 1934, October 20, 2002.

San Francisco Evening Post, October 20, 1894.

San Francisco Examiner, July 31, 1908, February 5, 1921, January 30, 1922, February 27, 1923, January 25, 1955.

Stockton Mail, January 30, 1908, July 20, 1908.

San Joaquin County Historical Museum, 111793 N. Micke Grove Rd., Lodi, California.

Siskiyou County Historical Society, Yreka, California.

Siskiyou County Genealogical Society, Marriages 1852-1910.

Society of California Pioneers, 300 4th Street, San Francisco, California.

Sunnyside Mausoleum, 4724 Cherry Street, Long Beach, California.

Sunset View Cemetery, 101 Colusa Ave., Berkeley, California.

Taylor, David Wooster, *Life of James Rolph Jr.,* (Committee for Publication of the Life of James Rolph Jr., January 1,1934).

Tutorow, Norman, *The Governor: The Life and Legacy of Leland Stanford, A California Colossus,* Vol. 1, Vol. II. (Spokane, Washington: The Arthur H. Clark Company, 2004).

United States Federal Census Record, 1860.

Wave, September 26, 1891, October 3, 1891.

Washington Post and Times *Herald, May 3, 1955.*

West Sacramento Archives, Betty Henderson Collection: Box: 8-13-377, Box: 8-31-877, Box: 8-10-311, Box: 8-10-377, Box: 8-15-877.

Woolridge, *History of the Sacramento Valley,* (Pioneer Historical Publishing, 1931), Vol. 1.

Endnotes

1   Rice, *The Women of Our Valley, 63-64.*
2   Lewis, *Pioneers of California, 95.*
3   Myers, *Ho for California, 9-20.*
4   Loc. Cit., 7.
5   *Sacramento Union, November 17,1873.*
6   *Sacramento Union,* January 9, 1856.
7   Internet, *www.witherells.com.*
8   California State Library, Bio File, John Downey.
9   *San Francisco Call,* January 21, 1883.
10   Melendy, *The Governors of California from Peter Burnett to Edmund G. Brown,* 132.
11   Sacramento History Journal, 2004/2005, 41.
12   Tutorow, *The Governor: The Life and Legacy of Leland Stanford a California Colossus, 882.*
13   St. Louis Missouri Historical Society, Letter.
14   *Alta California,* November 2, 1863.
15   Woolridge, *History of Sacramento Valley, 75.*
16   History of San Joaquin County, 580.
17   *Sacramento Union,* January 28, 1895.
18   Martin, *Stockton Album through the* Years, 221.
19   California State Library, Gillette Collection.
20   Gillette, *Gleanings and Weavings,* 8.
21   San Francisco Chronicle, January 26, 1955.
22   West Sacramento Archives, Betty Henderson Collection.
23   Ibid.

24   California State Library, Richardson Bio File.
25   *San Francisco Call, June 27, 1900.*
26   Taylor, *Life of James Rolph, Jr.,* 8.
27   West Sacramento Archives, Betty Henderson Collection.
28   *Sacramento Bee,* January 6, 1939.
29   West Sacramento Archives, Betty Henderson Collection.
30   Ibid.
31   Ibid.
32   Ibid.
33   Ibid.
34   Rarick, *The Life and Time of Pat Brown, California Rising,* 189.
35   West Sacramento Archives, Betty Henderson Collection.
36   Internet, *www.whitehouse.gov* /history/first ladies.
37   Internet, *www.reaganlibrary.com.*
38   Internet, *www.nationalreview.com.*
39   Internet, *www.mariashriver.com.*